W9-BTI-816

What Research Says to the Teacher

Questioning Skills, for Teachers

Second Edition

by William W. Wilen

nea **PROFESSIONAL LIBRARY**

National Education Association
Washington, D.C.

The Author
William W. Wilen is Associate Professor, Department of Teacher Development and Curriculum Studies, Kent State University, Ohio.

The Consultant
Gerald D. Bailey, Professor of Education, Kansas State University, Manhattan

The Advisory Panel
Olga Jane Beale, Elementary Coordinator, McAlester City Schools, Oklahoma

Libby Cohen, Assistant Professor of Education, University of Southern Maine, Gorham

Judi Horn, second grade teacher, Eldorado School, Spring Valley, New York

Mary C. Murphy, Professor of English, Springfield Technical Community College, Massachusetts

Douglas W. Scott, sixth grade teacher, Jordan Elementary School, Chandler, Arizona

Diane M. Stadler, Program Coordinator, Vacaville High School, California

Daniel Tharp, Head Teacher, Page Elementary School, Nebraska

David N. Wallace, History teacher, Memorial High School, Manchester, New Hampshire

Printing History
First Printing:	September 1982
Second Printing:	November 1984
SECOND EDITION:	January 1986
Fourth Printing:	February 1987
Fifth Printing:	July 1989

Note

The opinions expressed in this publication should not be construed as representing the policy or position of the National Education Association. Materials published as part of the What Research Says to the Teacher series are intended to be discussion documents for teachers who are concerned with specialized interests of the profession.

Library of Congress Cataloging in Publication Data

Wilen, William W.
    Questioning skills, for teachers.

    (What research says to the teacher)
    Bibliography: p.
    1. Questioning. I. Title.
LB1027.W527 1986   371.3'7   85-24054
ISBN 0-8106-1068-X

CONTENTS

AUTHOR'S PREFACE TO THE SECOND EDITION

The research reported since the publication of the first edition of this monograph continues to support the growing influence of teachers' questions and questioning techniques on student learning.

Several comprehensive reviews of research on questioning have implications for improving questioning skills. Dillon examined the nature of discussions and the role of questions (A).* He suggested that questions may inhibit student participation and that teachers should use alternative approaches, an idea that he developed in his book (B). Gall reviewed the research on the use of questions in recitation and found support for the effectiveness of that method (D). He recommended that students learn more about teacher questions and responding to them, and that teacher educators help teachers use recitation in their classrooms. In his review Wilen provided specific recommendations for teacher educators (L).

Several symposia at the 1985 meeting of the American Educational Research Association considered the significant contributions that researchers from many disciplines can make to questioning. All the papers analyzed five audiotaped secondary-level class sessions. Wilen reviewed several papers representing a pedagogical perspective (N). Roby identified five types of discussions in the taped episodes, each involving a variety of questions (G). Swift, Gooding, and Swift found that teachers needed greater understanding of basic discussion skills, including the use of wait time to stimulate student thinking (K). Francis reached a similar conclusion and found that students had not been trained in discussion skills (C). Wood and Wood found that teachers' questions served to control the group—the more questions teachers asked, the less initiative students took in asking questions or making comments (O). Russell concluded that, for the most part, teachers did not encourage students to provide rational support for their knowledge claims (H). The major implication of these studies is the need for pre- and in-service teacher training in skills for conducting effective discussions. An adaptation of the training program used by Schuck in his study might serve as a model to help accomplish this goal (I).

A continuing trend of the 1980s has been the attempt to identify specific questioning levels and techniques that impact student growth, particularly cognitive growth. Applying the meta-analytical technique to 20 previously conducted studies on the relationship between the level of teacher questioning and student achievement, Redfield and Rousseau found that the predominant use of higher-level questions led to gains in achievement (F). In addition, Wilen and Clegg in their synthesis of research findings identified several other questioning skills as positive correlates with achievement—phrasing, academic questions, low cognitive-level questions, wait time, probing of responses, and acknowledgment of correct responses (M).

Another area that has received increased attention is that of student-initiated questions. Research has suggested that such student involvement would reduce teacher control of discussions and thereby make students more effective learners. Hunkins proposed that teachers should help students devise questions within a planning, implementing, and assessing cycle (E). This would help reduce students' dependency on the teacher's authority and increase their opportunities for thinking. Steinbrink proposed several types of questions that students can learn to develop: descriptive, policy, opinion, and futures (J). More research in this alternative area is needed.

*See New Resources for the Second Edition on page 33.

INTRODUCTION

Since the turn of the century little disagreement has existed concerning the definition of questions or the variety of functions they can serve in the classroom. A question is broadly defined as any sentence having either an interrogative form or function. More precisely, teacher questions are instructional cues or "stimuli that convey the content elements to be learned and directions for what they are to do and how they are to do it" (75, p 26).* For example, "What is your opinion of the emphasis of the current economic policy?" and "Name the stages of photosynthesis." Both examples serve the function of instructional cues because they communicate content (current economic policy and photosynthesis) and direction (forming an opinion and recall) in both interrogative ("What is...?") and declarative ("Name the...") forms.

Because of the purpose they serve, questions have always been considered the "core of effective teaching" (56, 52). Over 120 years ago Ross suggested two major purposes for questions: to ascertain whether students understand and remember what has been taught and to have students apply what they have learned (92). These two purposes clearly illustrate the major differences between current theory and practice. Theory suggests that teachers should ask higher-cognitive-level questions to have students apply learnings, while practice demonstrates that teachers ask low-cognitive-level questions to check recall of knowledge.

This publication reviews the research findings related to the verbal questioning behaviors and practices of teachers. It emphasizes current research related to the impact of questioning practices on student thinking, achievement, and attitudes. This includes questioning techniques and strategies, and approaches to analyze classroom questions. Finally, it suggests an approach for teachers to use to gather information on their questioning behaviors in order to begin systematically improving their questioning practices.

DEVELOPMENT OF INTEREST IN QUESTIONING

Research on Questioning

From 1900 to 1950, the research on questioning was meager in quantity but significant in that findings provided an awareness of teachers' questioning behaviors (104, 21, 5, 22, 23, 24, 27). Stevens, who conducted the first major systematic research in 1912, found

---

*Numbers in parentheses in the text refer to the Bibliography beginning on page 27.

that approximately 80 percent of the average school day was occupied with teacher questions and student answers. Teachers verbalized about 64 percent of the time and asked about two to four questions per minute. Students were expected to recall facts, but not necessarily to engage in thinking above the memory level. Stevens concluded that if instruction were to improve, teachers must develop questions that stimulate reflective thinking (104).

Beginning with the Stevens study, describing teachers' questioning behaviors became an area of research. For the most part, researchers' findings supported the discovery of low-cognitive-level questions (21, 5, 22). Three developments during the 1950's and 1960's stimulated renewed interest and further research in this area. First, increased attention to intellectual achievements developed following the successful Soviet launch of Sputnik in 1957. Fearing that our academic programs were inferior to those of other countries, the federal government supported the development of a wide range of curriculum projects. The instructional strategies required to teach the new curricula emphasized the development of students' higher thought processes. These strategies, such as inquiry, relied heavily on the teacher's ability to stimulate critical and creative thinking skills through effective questioning behaviors (31).

Second, to study teaching directly, researchers applied systematic observation techniques in classrooms to objectively describe and analyze teacher behaviors. Starting with Flanders' Interaction Analysis and Amidon and Hunter's Verbal Interaction Category System, many of these instruments included categories intended to gather objective data on teachers' questioning behaviors in order to determine effectiveness (40, 1, 31).

And third, the research of Bloom and Guilford gave impetus to major efforts to identify and classify components of the cognitive operation in the classroom. Despite the different intentions of these researchers—devising categories of intellectual operations—their models served to stimulate valuable research into the cognitive aspects of classroom interaction—especially the questioning behaviors of teachers. Sanders, and Gallagher and Aschner successfully adapted the categories of Bloom and Guilford, respectively, to produce systematic approaches that effectively identify the cognitive levels of teacher questions in the classroom setting (9, 54, 96, 48, 31).

From 1950 to 1970 research on teachers' questioning behaviors went through a transition. The focus on identifying the cognitive emphasis of questions continued. The major change was researchers' use of increasingly sophisticated methods of systematic observation. Another thrust was devising and testing training programs using systematic observation techniques to provide pre-service and in-service teachers with questioning skills. The training focused primarily on raising questioning levels to better conform to desired student thought levels. Other research efforts began to determine the impact of teacher questioning behaviors on student learning outcomes. This research continues and will continue well into the 1980's largely because of public concern for teacher accountability.

Current Research Trends

The current period of research activity on questioning began with several major reviews of studies conducted since the turn of the century. Hoetker and Ahlbrand concluded that classroom verbal behavior patterns, as indicated by research dating back to 1912, have been extremely stable. Concerning the finding that teachers have persisted in asking low-cognitive-level questions, the authors challenged the theorists by suggesting that teachers may be right in continually using the recitation method (59). Gall concluded after his review that training teachers to improve questioning practices should now become the focus of research because the function of questions is to produce desired changes in student behavior (42). Determining the impact of teacher questions on student learning outcomes is the major emphasis of questioning research today. In his review of correlational studies of teaching skills and student achievement, Rosenshine found no clear relationship between higher-level questioning and student achievement. He did, however, find a possible relationship of certain questioning skills (high interaction and probing) to achievement (89).

The phases of research on questioning parallel the cycles of research on teaching effectiveness described by Rosenshine, and, to an extent, Medley. The first two cycles identifying teacher characteristics and systematically observing teacher behavior have provided a transition to the third phase. The concern of researchers now focuses on the specific questioning levels and skills that have an impact on student growth, particularly cognitive growth (91, 78).

These research findings are discussed in more detail in the next two sections of this book, "Teachers' Questioning Practices" and "Impact of Questioning on Learning Outcomes."

TEACHERS' QUESTIONING PRACTICES

Function of Questions

The questions teachers regularly ask reflect their short- and long-range decisions about students, instruction, and curriculum. In a very basic sense, the kinds of questions teachers ask and the techniques they employ to interact with students imply their philosophy of instruction. Most of the decisions teachers make about questioning in the classroom are intuitive and are therefore based primarily on experience. But effective teaching reflects effective decisionmaking. In their instructional planning, then, teachers need to give careful consideration to the questions to be asked and the interaction patterns to be developed in order to facilitate student achievement of learning outcomes.

Although the two major enduring purposes of teacher questions are to determine student understanding of basic facts associated with specific content and to have students apply facts using critical and creative thinking skills, educators have advocated other related purposes: (1) to stimulate student participation; (2) to initiate a review of material previously read or studied; (3) to initiate discussion of a topic, issue, or problem based on previous learnings; (4) to involve students in creative thinking; (5) to diagnose student abilities; (6) to evaluate student preparation for a learning task; (7) to determine to what extent objectives have been achieved; (8) to arouse student interest; (9) to control student behavior; and (10) to support student contributions in class (17, 53, 66).

This variety of functions suggests the important role questions can play in instruction. It is not difficult to imagine a teacher using many of the questioning behaviors in a single lesson. A high school art teacher, for example, can arouse student interest by showing a slide of Dali's *Soft Construction with Boiled Beans. Premonition of Civil War* and asking, "What's your impression of this painting?" Higher-level thinking can be stimulated further with "What message might the artist be attempting to communicate in this work?" The teacher can then follow this divergent thinking with review questions focusing on the specifics of the Spanish Civil War which the class has been studying as part of an interdisciplinary World History and Art unit. Lower-level convergent thinking can be stimulated with these questions: "Who was the leader of the Nationalists who later became head of the Spanish government?" and "Why did Germany and Italy get involved?" Other questions directed to one or two students can serve to diagnose difficulties they may have had in understanding the impact of war on people. At any point, a question may be necessary to manage a student's behavior by involving him/her in the learning activity ("Gregg, how does the conflict between the Protestants and Catholics in Ireland affect the feelings of your pen pal in Belfast?"). Or a question can support a student's previous contribution ("What did Terri mention yesterday concerning her father's feelings about the Vietnam War?"). The teacher can close this discussion about one artist's representation of the horrors of war with a question designed to stimulate creative thinking: "What title would you give this piece?"

According to educational theorists, the purposes of questions are

8

clear, but what do teachers consider these purposes to be? Pate and Bremer administered a questionnaire to 190 elementary teachers (grades 1-6) asking for the three most important purposes of teacher questions. Eight-six percent of the teachers stated the purpose was to "check on effectiveness of teaching by checking on pupils' learning"; 54 percent said "diagnosis"; 47 percent said "check on pupils" recall of specific facts"; and only 10 percent said "require pupils to use fact in generalizing and in making inferences" (84, p. 418). Teachers clearly do not consider a major purpose of their questions to be to stimulate higher-level student thinking.

Questioning Techniques

For over 120 years much advice has been offered concerning questioning techniques for teachers to use during recitations and discussions. The advice has generally remained the same. In his 100-year review of British methods texts, McNamara found that information about questions has remained consistent. He proposed several reasons: teachers' questioning skills are "common sense" and therefore endure; methods texts, not often updated, tend to be redundant; and the number of statements one can offer about questioning is limited (77). Good and Brophy caution, however, that much of the advice on effective questioning techniques is based more on logic than on research (50). This suggests researchers' uncertainty about the most effective techniques—those that facilitate learning outcomes. Ladas and Osti realistically conclude, though, that teachers cannot wait until the research findings validate specific techniques; they need the best advice available now (72).

Table 1 contains a list of techniques synthesized from a variety of works dealing exclusively or in part with questioning.

Questioning Strategies

Just as many books and articles deal with questioning techniques, many publications, although fewer in number, expand the treatment of questioning methods into strategies. According to Hyman, a strategy is a "carefully prepared plan involving a sequence of steps designed to achieve a given goal" (66, p. xiii). It serves as a guide for the teacher to determine which questions to plan and ask in the classroom. It provides a framework for interaction with students. Without a strategy, a discussion can become a series of single questions lacking cohesion and purposeful sequence. Although the teacher must remain flexible and ready to respond to unpredictable interaction sequences, Hyman suggests that teacher effectiveness as a strategic questioner is based on the ability to manage the interaction by combining the individual questions into a pattern designed to

Table 1
QUESTIONING TECHNIQUES

1. *Plan key questions to provide lesson structure and direction.* Write them into lesson plans, at least one for each objective—especially higher-level questions. Ask some spontaneous questions based on student responses (50, 53, 67, 96, 113).

2. *Phrase questions clearly and specifically.* Avoid vague or ambiguous questions such as "What did we learn yesterday?" or "What about the heroine of the story?" Ask single questions; avoid run-on questions that lead to student frustration and confusion. Clarity increases probability of accurate responses (25, 50, 53, 67).

3. *Adapt questions to student ability level.* This enhances understanding and reduces anxiety. For heterogeneous classes, phrase questions in natural, simple language, adjusting vocabulary and sentence structure to students' language and conceptual levels (50, 53).

4. *Ask questions logically and sequentially.* Avoid random questions lacking clear focus and intent. Consider students' intellectual ability, prior understanding of content, topic, and lesson objective(s). Asking questions in a planned sequence will enhance student thinking and learning (50, 53).

5. *Ask questions at variety of levels.* Use knowledge-level questions to determine basic understandings and to serve as a basis for higher-level thinking. Higher-level questions provide students opportunities to practice higher forms of thought (50, 53, 67, 113).

6. *Follow up student responses.* Develop a response repertoire that encourages students to clarify initial responses, lift thought to higher levels, and support a point of view or opinion. For example, "Can you restate that?" "Could you clarify that further?" "What are some alternatives?" "How can you defend your position?" Encourage students to clarify, expand, or support initial responses to higher-level questions (25, 67, 113).

7. *Give students time to think when responding.* Increase wait time after asking a question to three to five seconds to increase number and length of student responses and to encourage higher-level thinking. Insisting upon instantaneous responses significantly decreases probability of meaningful interaction with and among students. Allow sufficient wait time before repeating or rephrasing questions to ensure student understanding (17, 50, 53, 67, 94).

8. *Use questions that encourage wide student participation.* Distribute questions to involve majority of students in learning activities. For example, call on nonvolunteers, using discretion for difficulty level of questions. Be alert for reticent students' verbal and nonverbal cues such as perplexed look or partially raised hand. Encourage student-to-student interaction. Use circular or semicircular seating to create environment conducive to increased student involvement (17, 25, 50, 53, 113).

9. *Encourage student questions.* This encourages active participation. Student questions at higher cognitive levels stimulate higher levels of thought, essential for inquiry approach. Give students opportunities to formulate questions and carry out followup investigations of interest. Facilitate group and independent inquiry with a supportive social-emotional climate, using praise and encouragement, accepting and applying student ideas, responding to student feelings, and actively promoting student involvement in all phases of learning (17, 64, 67, 113).

achieve an objective (66).

Before devising or selecting a questioning strategy, teachers should first consider the function of the strategy. Hunkins suggests four major functions for grouping questions into strategies: centering, expansion, distribution, and order (65). The centering function guides the teachers in focusing students' attention on the learning material at a particular cognitive level. This function is especially appropriate at the beginning of a lesson when the teacher has students focus on the topic, problem, or issue. Centering can occur at any cognitive level. For example, a teacher reads a newspaper account of a woman, employed by the ABC Electronics Company, who has recently brought a lawsuit against the company charging discrimination in promotion practices. A centering question to initiate inquiry on the article is "What are the facts in this case?"; a higher-level, followup question, "What do you perceive to be the problem?" Other centering questions that can help guide the investigation are "What terms need to be clarified?" and "What are some data sources you could use to gather information?" (65).

The expansion function helps students extend their thought at the same cognitive level or raise it to another level. Using the illustrative lesson, the following questions extend divergent thinking: "What are some other factors that might cause high officials in ABC Electronics to purposely keep women from advancing in rank?" and "Are there some other value conflicts to consider?" Expansion questions lifting students' thinking to higher levels include "Now that you have gathered and analyzed some data, can you offer any tentative solutions?" and "Of the ideas you have presented to help ABC Electronics eliminate discriminatory practices, which do you think best?" (65).

The distributive function, along with the ordering function, is used with the centering and expansion functions. Its purpose is to encourage as many students as possible to participate in the learning activity. Questions serving this function are "Judy, what do you think of Neal's opinion?" and "Fred, you've uncovered some interesting information. Could you share it with Marlene because she is having some trouble locating data on this aspect of the problem?" (65).

The order function physically manages and emotionally supports students in order to maintain an appropriate classroom atmosphere. Questions to physically order the class and promote the inquiry process include "What rules must students follow when using the instructional resources center?" and "If you continue acting that way, how will it affect the others in your group?" A question providing emotional support: "You seem to be having a problem. What can I do to help you locate the information?" (65).

In a series of three books, Weil, Joyce, and Kluwin offer teachers the knowledge and skills to apply eight alternative instructional strategies: concept attainment (13), inquiry training (105), advance organizer (4), synectics (51), the nondirective model (88); role-playing (98), the jurisprudential model (82), and social simulation (11). These strategies are organized into three families of teaching models—information processing, social, and personal—and each strategy represents distinct assumptions about student learning and teachers' instructional roles. Each one is interactive—that is, teachers ask questions and students respond to achieve specific objectives—and the relationship of the effective use of questions to selected strategies is evident (110, 109, 108).

Analyzing Questions

The systematic observation and analysis of classroom interaction is a relatively recent phenomenon. Anderson developed one of the first systems when he investigated the dominative and integrative behavior of teachers (2). Subsequent efforts by Withall and Flanders contributed greatly to understanding teacher and student behaviors that influence classroom and social-emotional climate (118, 40).

Teacher questioning behavior is analyzed through observation and collection of objective data on such aspects of questions as cognitive level, length, and frequency. Systematic observation techniques can also record and categorize the verbalizations preceding and following questions as well as many characteristics of student responses (99). One of the more recent reviews of this topic identified 21 classification systems for classroom questions (87). Most focused on the cognitive levels.

Although questions were formally classified according to cognitive levels as early as 1860, not until the Stevens study in 1912 were they categorized for research purposes. This study classified questions recorded by stenographers according to those stimulating memory and reflection, with particular emphasis on those eliciting comparisons and judgments from students (104). Not until the middle 1950's through the efforts of Bloom and Guilford were researchers provided explicit criteria for identifying and analyzing classroom thinking operations. The purpose of Bloom's research was to provide a classification scheme of the intended goals of education, with emphasis on developing educational objectives in the cognitive domain. He identified six major hierarchical classes of objectives, or educational behaviors, ranging from simple to complex intellectual abilities and skills: knowledge, comprehension, application, analysis, synthesis, and evaluation (9). Sanders adapted Bloom's classification to his study of questions by dividing the comprehension category into translation and interpretation because of the distinct kinds of thinking involved, and retitling the knowledge category "memory" (96).

During the period that Bloom devised his Taxonomy, Guilford developed his Structure of Intellect model, classifying intellectual factors several ways. One basis of classification is by the mental operations performed broken down into five major groups: cognition, memory, convergent thinking, divergent thinking, and evaluation (54). Based on Guilford's model, Gallagher and Aschner constructed a category system to examine teacher-student classroom interaction. Their major adaptation was to combine the cognition and memory categories because of the similarity of mental operations required:

1. Cognitive-Memory—students mentally reproduce facts, formulas, or other remembered content through use of such processes as recognition, rote memory, and selective recall.
2. Convergent Thinking—students analyze and integrate given or remembered data. The outcome is one expected end result or answer because of the tightly structured framework through which the individual must respond.
3. Divergent Thinking—students generate independently their own information within a data-poor situation, or take a new direction or perspective on a given topic.
4. Evaluative Thinking—students deal with matters of judgment, value, and choice. (48, pp. 186-88)

Table 2 contains sample questions teachers might ask in their classrooms categorized according to the Sanders and the Gallagher-Aschner systems. Because the convergent thinking category of the Gallagher-Aschner system is so broad, encompassing four categories of the Sanders system (translation, interpretation, application, and analysis), an adaptation was made classifying questions as low convergent and high convergent. The primary difference is that analysis questions are higher level and therefore stimulate more open-ended student responses (95).

To simplify question classification and make self-analysis of teacher behavior easier, Enokson devised an approach that combines the principles of the Bloom and Guilford systems (35). The main advantage of this approach over other systems, including Bloom's and Guilford's, is that it requires little formal training to learn and apply the categories. Teachers can classify a question according to two separate parameters: cognition, based on Bloom's Taxonomy and nature, based on Guilford's structure of intellect. Both parameters are considered interrelated and function simultaneously at different levels. Thus, questions can be classified according to their nature and cognition as convergent-low, convergent-high, divergent-low, and divergent-high, depending on whether facts are recalled or integrated and whether the question has only one possible answer or

Table 2
SAMPLE QUESTIONS CATEGORIZED ACCORDING TO SANDERS
AND GALLAGHER-ASCHNER (ADAPTED) SYSTEMS

QUESTION	SYSTEM	
	Sanders based on Bloom	Gallagher-Aschner (based on Guilford)
Who invented the sewing machine?	Memory	Cognitive-Memory
What is the definition for photosynthesis?....	Memory	Cognitive-Memory
How many colors are on the chart?	Memory	Cognitive-Memory
In your own words, according to the story, how did the dog get loose?...............	Translation	Convergent (Low)
How would you say this in German?	Translation	Convergent (Low)
What is the meaning of this political cartoon?.............................	Translation	Convergent (Low)
How would you compare the climates of Miami and San Francisco?..............	Interpretation	Convergent (Low)
What are the similarities between these two points of view?	Interpretation	Convergent (Low)
How are these three members related?.......	Interpretation	Convergent (Low)
According to our definition of revolution, which of the following conflicts would be considered revolutions?	Application	Convergent (Low)
How would you solve this problem using the accounting procedure provided?	Application	Convergent (Low)
What is an example of cooperation in your home?........................	Application	Convergent (Low)
Why did the girl run away from home?	Analysis	Convergent (High)
Now that you have completed the experiment, what is your conclusion as to why the substance became denser?...............	Analysis	Convergent (High)
What evidence can you provide to support your view that the constitutional power of the president has diminished over the years? ...	Analysis	Convergent (High)
How can we raise money to support the recycling center?	Synthesis	Divergent
Suppose that England had won the American War for Independence, how might pioneers' movement to the west have been affected? .	Synthesis	Divergent
What is a good title for this story?	Synthesis	Divergent
Did you think the plot of this novel was well developed?........................	Evaluation	Evaluation
What is your favorite orchestral instrument? .	Evaluation	Evaluation
How would you rate the effectiveness of the Environmental Protection Agency?........	Evaluation	Evaluation

14

different possible answers (35). Table 3 contains examples of questions illustrating the application of this model.

Table 3
SAMPLE QUESTIONS
CATEGORIZED ACCORDING TO ENOKSON'S SYSTEM

QUESTION	CLASSIFICATION
What is the definition of pollution?....................	Convergent-low
Based on the account of a hypothetical city you have just read, which form of pollution most seriously threatens the people?.............	Convergent-high
What are some of the approaches suggested by the EPA to solve major air pollution problems?..........	Divergent-low
How might we devise a plan to significantly reduce the city's air pollution problem?..............	Divergent-high

Knowledge and skill in classifying questions can help teachers determine the degree of student thinking being stimulated. This identification and subsequent analysis can ultimately help them ascertain if course goals and lesson objectives are being met.

Types of Teacher Questions

Although a wide range of questioning is possible and recommended, research has consistently demonstrated teacher preference for low-cognitive-level questions typically categorized at the memory level. Since Stevens's first systematic study on questioning (104), this finding has been verified at all grade levels in a variety of subject areas.

Floyd classified the verbal questioning behavior of 40 elementary teachers and found them asking 93 percent of all classroom questions. Forty-two percent of the questions were on the memory level; only 6 percent stimulated high-level thinking (41). Observing 14 science lessons in five elementary schools, Moyer concluded that teachers are consistent in the types of questions they ask and are not encouraging critical thinking in their classes (81). This finding was supported by Blosser's review of observational studies of science classrooms: science teachers operate primarily at the cognitive-memory level at both the elementary and secondary levels (10). (See sample questions in Table 2.)

Investigating the question levels of reading teachers in second, fourth, and sixth grade classrooms, Guszak found the greatest portion were on the recall and recognition levels with emphasis on literal comprehension (55). In a junior-high-level study of teacher-pupil interaction in English classes, Hudgins and Ahlbrand found students operating at the cognitive-memory level 80 percent of the time (62).

At the secondary level, Gallagher studied 235 students in junior high and high school gifted classes, and concluded that the basis of classroom discourse was at the cognitive-memory level. The next most frequently used level was the convergent level (47). (See sample questions in Table 2.)

Observing secondary school social studies student teachers, Davis and Tinsley found the emphasis on the memory level and more questions at this level than at all others combined. These researchers found the conclusions distressing because of the assumed emphasis of critical thinking in the social studies (29). In their three-year study of social studies student teachers, Barth and Shermis found only 14 of 30 student teachers taped before and after student teaching asking questions associated with the inquiry process—even though they had received training in inquiry teaching. The authors hypothesized that, despite experience with higher-level questioning and inquiry strategies in their methods courses, the student teachers may not have fully comprehended the theory of inquiry (reflective) teaching. They also hypothesized that the student teachers may not have been supported by their supervising teachers in their efforts to demonstrate higher-level questioning (6).

The overall conclusion that teachers have persisted in using low-cognitive-level, primarily memory, questions aplies also to the questions used for lesson plans and examinations. Pfeiffer and Davis categorized the questions contained in teacher-made semester examinations for all ninth grade courses at one junior high school, concluding, "The teacher-made examinations . . . clearly emphasized the objective of knowledge acquisition and the mental process of memory." (85, 10). In another study, 67 student teachers, upon completing their experience, composed discussion and test questions for hypothetical eighth and eleventh grade American history classes. When the questions were categorized, the data revealed no differentiation in the questions planned for tests and discussions, or in those planned for junior and senior high school students. Moreover, more evaluation and memory questions were planned than all other types. Thus, the authors concluded that questions composed for secondary school students provided very little variety or opportunity to engage in critical thinking processes and skills (107).

IMPACT OF QUESTIONING
ON LEARNING OUTCOMES

Student Thinking

Ever since the first studies of teacher-student interaction were conducted, a major assumption of educators and researchers has been that a direct and positive relationship exists between the cognitive levels of teacher questions and the thinking levels of student responses. The research findings on this presumed relationship are mixed, however.

Taba's research project studied the developmental effects of a specially designed curriculum and instructional program on student thinking skills. She found that teaching strategies which involved extensive questioning were the most important single influence on students' cognitive performance. Specifically, the research data clearly demonstrated that "the nature of the questions has a singular impact on the progression of thought in the class. The questions teachers ask set the limits within which students can operate and the expectations regarding the lack of cognitive operations." (106, p. 177). At about the same period, Gallagher and Aschner were attempting to identify and describe the kinds of thinking exhibited in the classroom. Using gifted students at the junior and senior high levels, they found the basis of classroom discourse to be cognitive-memory-level teacher questions and student responses. As for higher-level thinking, they found that a 5 percent increase in divergent-level questions initiated a 40 percent increase in divergent responses from students. Their conclusion: the teacher controls the thought levels in the classroom (48, 47). More recently, a study of student teachers in elementary science by Arnold, Atwood, and Rogers also found the question level significantly related to the response level (3).

The results of two other studies were inconsistent with these findings (71, 79). Exposing students to three treatments of 65 percent higher-level teacher questions, 50 percent higher- and lower-level questions, and 65 percent lower-level questions, Konya found that students responded more often at higher levels when teachers asked equal amounts of higher- and lower-level questions (71). More recently, Mills and others reanalyzing the data from an earlier study (43) found only about a 50 percent relationship between teacher questions and student responses. Mills concluded, "The result provides a firm basis for dispelling the belief that there is a high correlation between types of teacher questions and types of student answers. It appears that training teachers to ask higher cognitive questions is not adequate in itself to insure comparable levels of student cognitive performance." (79, p. 200).

In response to the recent finding that question and response levels are not highly related, Winne and Marx suggest that student perceptions of the thinking required by higher cognitive questions differ from teacher intentions as indicated by the questions asked (116). If this is the case, it could very easily result in a lack of relationship between responses and questions. Mills and others recommended training teachers to incorporate interaction techniques focusing on verbal cues to help students become aware of the thought processes required to respond appropriately. Further, they suggested training students in an approach to question classification to help them more easily play the higher cognitive discussion "game" (79).

Essential to student thinking, especially at the higher cognitive levels, is the time the teacher allots for the student to respond after asking a question. Stevens reported a lack of pausing skills, commonly called "wait time," "think time," and "lapse time." The teachers she investigated asked questions at a rate of two to three per minute (104, p. 16).

Concern for the time allotted students to reflect before responding to teacher questions prompted Rowe to investigate wait time. In the first part of the study, Rowe found the mean wait time to be one second after the teacher asked a question and the student responded. If the student did not respond in one second, the teacher either repeated or rephrased the question, asked another question, or called on another student. After receiving a response, the average teacher waited only 0.9 seconds before reacting or asking another question (94).

The second part of Rowe's study demonstrated the potential of wait time as an important teacher skill to aid students' higher cognitive processes. After teachers had been trained to increase their wait time to three to five seconds, Rowe's analysis of over 900 tapes of these teachers produced the following conclusions: (1) increased length of student responses; (2) increased number of unsolicited appropriate responses; (3) decreased number of failures to respond; (4) increased student confidence in responding; (5) increased speculative thinking; (6) decreased teacher-centered teaching, increased student-student interaction; (7) more student-provided evidence preceding or following inference statements; (8) increased number of student questions; (9) increased contributions of slow students; (10) increased variety of student structuring, soliciting, and reacting moves. Rowe also found that teachers developed greater response flexibility, changed the number and kind of questions they used, and tended to wait longer for responses from more capable students (94). Recently Hassler supported these findings in language arts (58).

Based on efforts at the University of Maryland Reading Clinic to increase the amount of wait time, Gambrell suggests several steps for teachers to consider:

1. *Teacher preparation.* Silently count up to five seconds after asking a question to help establish a routine to use wait time.
2. *Student preparation.* Tell students that wait time will be extended.
3. *Begin slowly.* At first, plan to use wait time during a specific part of a lesson, especially a part emphasizing higher-level thinking (49).

Student Achievement

A major concern of teachers today is the impact of their verbal and written questions on student learning outcomes as measured primarily by achievement tests. Only within the last two decades have a growing number of studies provided some tentative conclusions.

Very few studies have compared the effects of written and oral teacher questions. In a study involving 179 high school students, Rothkopf found better instructional results obtained from students who were questioned by teachers during individual study time compared to those who responded to written questions from a science text (93). In his review of the literature, Hargie concluded that teachers' oral questions are more effective than written questions (57).

Another important area is the relationship of the frequency of teacher questions and student learning. In his first major review of correlational studies on teaching behaviors and student achievement, Rosenshine found that a high frequency of interaction related significantly to achievement. But he did not find a relationship between higher-level questions and achievement (89). This conclusion is puzzling considering some of the research that seemed to support the positive relationship between higher-level teacher questions and high-level student responses. In a later study, Rosenshine found further support for the lack of relationship between the frequency of higher-level questions and achievement. Additionally, the frequency of factual single-answer questions was positively related to student achievement. This finding was based on studies that focused on basic skill instruction in reading and mathematics for first through fifth graders (91). Good and Brophy offered three reasons for the relationship between the frequency of low-level questions and learning gains: (1) teachers who have high frequencies of questions plan and organize well, and therefore have few classroom management problems; (2) they heavily involve their students in academic activities leaving little time for them to pursue nonacademic goals; (3) they probably also involve their students in a variety of oral participation instructional approaches (50).

Although the frequency of higher-level questions appears unrelated to achievement, several studies found that verbalized higher-level questions lead to greater achievement than do low-level questions. Kleinman studied 23 teachers and their seventh and eighth grade general science students to determine, in part, whether the kinds of teacher questions influence student understanding of science. She found that students of teachers who asked higher-level critical thinking questions performed better on a science achievement test than students of teachers who asked questions requiring recall of information (69). Also using junior high science teachers and students (ninth grade), Ladd found that teachers who asked a greater proportion of higher inquiry questions, as compared to those who asked low inquiry questions, caused greater change in student achievement as indicated on a posttest composed of low and high inquiry questions (73). Investigating the relationship between knowledge-level and higher-level social studies questions and achievement on tests, Buggey concluded that significantly greater achievement was made by second grade students in the treatment group whose teachers asked 70 percent higher-level questions and 30 percent knowledge-level questions (14). Savage found no differences in his replication of Buggey's study with fifth graders. He concluded that at the fifth grade level, students' thought was not as dependent upon teacher questioning style as it was at the second grade level (97).

Three more recent studies of middle-school-age students produced mixed conclusions about the positive influence of higher-level questioning. Gall and others, using sixth grade classes, found that treatment group teachers asking 25 percent higher cognitive questions outperformed two other groups using 50 percent and 75 percent higher cognitive questions on knowledge acquisition and higher cognitive written and oral tests. Discussions guided by 50 percent higher cognitive questions were found to be the least effective in stimulating recall of information (45). Wilson examined the processing strategies of average and below-average sixth and seventh grade readers in response to factual and inferential questions. She found that average readers outperformed below-average readers in response to inferential questions but not in response to factual questions on the majority of reading passages (115). In the third study, Evenson found that treatments of 70 percent higher-cognitive-level questions facilitated fifth and sixth graders' recall of content but were ineffective in developing higher-level understandings. She also found that student achievement was significantly better in competitive instructional environments as compared to cooperative environments (36). Evenson's second finding tends to support Kniep and Grossman's conclusion that fifth graders in competitive instructional environments performed better on high-cognitive-level tests than students in cooperative environments. In both environments teachers asked high-level questions and student achievement was measured at the recall and higher cognitive levels (70).

As with any relatively new area of educational research, studies with opposing findings can be expected. During the past decade several investigators have examined the research on the relationship of teaching behaviors and student achievement focusing on the impact of teachers' questioning behaviors. Rosenshine followed up his earlier review of correlational studies (89) with an in-depth review of three major studies on classroom instruction (90). Although he found no clear relationship between teacher use of higher-cognitive-level questions and student achievement in 1971, data from three extensive studies conducted by other researchers (102, 103, 12) since then led him to conclude that there was a positive relationship between lower-cognitive-level questions and achievement and a lack of a relationship between higher-level questions and achievement. The common aspect of these three studies was the use of primary grade teachers with low socioeconomic-status students and an emphasis on learning outcome measures in reading and mathematics (90). In 1979 Rosenshine expanded his interpretation of the findings of the three studies by concluding that "open-ended questions, questions about personal experience, and questions about opinions were negatively correlated with achievement" (91, p. 45).

In another view, Winne carefully examined 18 studies of preschoolers through twelfth graders in a variety of subject areas to determine if teacher use of higher cognitive questions was related to student achievement. According to Winne, the findings "indicate that whether teachers use predominantly higher cognitive questions or predominantly fact questions makes little difference in student achievement" (117, p. 43). He suggested that more research is needed on the impact of higher cognitive questions on student cognitive processes.

After a teacher asks a question and a student responds, several followup options are available. The teacher can reward the student positively or negatively depending on whether the response is acceptable or unacceptable; probe with a followup question to encourage the student to restate or clarify, elaborate, expand, or support the response; redirect the question to another volunteering or nonvolunteering student; or ask a related question. Very little research has been conducted on the impact of teacher followup questions on student outcomes and the findings that are available are mixed.

In a study of third graders, Wright and Nuthall found a significant positive relationship between teacher questions asked one at a time and achievement. Students of teachers who asked two or more questions without a pause did not achieve as well (119). In a recent

21

study, Land found teacher clarity significantly related to student achievement on a test made up of low-level questions (74). Wright and Nuthall also found a positive relationship between the percentage of teacher questions answered by students and achievement. Negatively correlated with achievement was the frequency with which teachers provided information immediately following their own questions. The frequency of teachers' probing questions requiring students to elaborate, expand, or explain responses, according to Wright and Nuthall, had no relationship to achievement. But the frequency of questions redirected to other students was significantly related to achievement (119). Using sixth graders, Gall and others supported the findings that probing did not relate to achievement, but they also found, in contradiction, that redirection did not increase achievement or higher-cognitive-level oral or written responses (45).

Student Attitudes

The learning outcome receiving the least attention by educational researchers—concerning the impact of teacher questioning behavior—is student attitudes. Students may reflect their disposition toward responding to teacher questions at a variety of cognitive levels, as well as toward teacher use of specific questioning techniques, in their feelings, opinions, and preferences. For example, students with a negative attitude toward teacher questioning behaviors may possibly exhibit it in their behavioral patterns, academic performance, and/or perception of teacher and subject.

Several studies have investigated the influence of the discussion method on student attitudes, and student preferences for the cognitive levels of teacher questions. Fisher found that reading literature changed fifth graders' attitudes toward the topic (Indians), and involving students in a discussion after reading significantly increased attitude change more than reading alone (38). Gall and others also found a relationship between questions and the positive attitudes of sixth graders. Using six attitude measures, these researchers found written and discussion questions equally effective in stimulating positive attitudes toward the topic (ecology) and toward discussion as an instructional method. They also found that higher cognitive questions did not affect student attitudes (44).

Considering preferences a major indication of student attitudes, Wilen investigated student preferences for the cognitive levels of their teachers' verbal questioning behavior and the relationship of preferences to test score gains. In this study, American history students were exposed to four treatments of questioning corresponding to the Gallagher-Aschner question levels. Students failed to indicate a preference for higher-level questions, and those who preferred low-level questions performed best on written tests incorporating such questions. Wilen concludes that students must develop positive attitudes toward higher-level questioning if instructional approaches such as inquiry are to be effective (112, 114).

IMPROVING QUESTIONING PRACTICES

Once the importance of teacher questions as a stimulus to student thinking and learning was realized, the development of instructional improvement programs to acquaint and train pre-service and in-service teachers in questioning skills was inevitable. This thrust became apparent during the 1960's when research efforts had convincingly demonstrated that teacher questions persistently demanded primarily low-cognitive-level thinking. Thus, researchers and teacher educators, and later some commercial producers, devised instructional improvement programs to train teachers to increase question frequency, raise cognitive emphasis, phrase questions properly, develop probing and redirection skills, and increase wait time. These training programs often incorporated typescripts of classroom dialogues, simulations of teaching, and audio and video-tapes to provide realism in identifying, analyzing, and practicing questioning behaviors.

Many researchers and educators have been generally successful in their attempts to change teachers' questioning behaviors, especially in raising cognitive levels. Although Houston conducted one of the first successful in-service training programs in the 1930's (61), it was not until the 1960's that a wide range of effective training programs was developed and tested. Using Bloom's Taxonomy to introduce the cognitive levels, Clegg and his associates found that in-service and student teachers significantly altered their questioning behaviors by achieving higher cognitive levels in the classroom (20, 37). Also using Bloom's Taxonomy in an individualized in-service approach, Zoch found that his experimental group of kindergarten and first grade teachers asked a greater percentage of higher-level questions (121). Using videotaped lessons as the means of instruction with Gallagher and Aschner's classification scheme, Cunningham found that pre-service elementary science teachers significantly decreased the proportion of cognitive-memory-level questions and significantly increased the proportion of divergent-level questions after instruction (26). After an in-service program on questioning skills, Psencik found American history teachers asking more above-memory-level questions (86). Crump developed and used learning packages to successfully alter intermediate social studies teachers' oral and written questioning behaviors (28). More recently, Wright found a microteaching program the most effective technique for secondary methods students to increase questioning levels (120).

Not all training programs have been equally successful. Douce trained an experimental group of first through tenth grade teachers in questioning techniques using learning packages. After instruction, the teachers did not ask significantly more or higher-level questions. Douce concluded that teachers with experience found it more difficult to change their questioning behaviors than did student teachers (34). In another program, Welch found that social studies student teachers asked fewer higher-level questions after reading and being tested on Sanders's approach to question classification (111).

The Far West Laboratory for Educational Research and Development has produced and successfully tested a program available to teachers to assist in developing questioning skills. This minicourse is a self-contained in-service training program that uses, in part, microteaching. Several versions have been produced and found effective (42). Using the minicourse approach, Pagliaro trained student teachers and cooperating teachers to determine if the questioning behaviors of the former changed as a result of placement with the latter. She found that student teachers who displayed low scoring levels of questioning behaviors prior to their student teaching experience, scored significantly higher when placed with cooperating teachers who displayed high scoring levels of questioning behaviors (83). Buttery and Michalak also used the minicourse approach to train elementary-level student teachers. Using a clinical supervision process, they found the experimental group significantly improved in eleven questioning skill areas, as compared with a control group that improved in only two areas (16). In another interesting study, Malvern found that students of in-service teachers with training in the minicourse approach improved their inferential thinking skills over students of teachers without such training (76).

Realizing that a systematic approach to improving instruction can be threatening when conducted by those outside the classroom, and can also be time-consuming, Kindsvatter and Wilen developed a practical and effective approach for teachers. The Improving Classroom Instruction (ICI) approach focuses on a variety of instructional skill areas, including cognitive levels and phrasing of questions. Teachers can use it as either a shared-analysis approach with a colleague, or a self-analysis approach in conjunction with a video or audiotape recording. The self-analysis approach is a particularly nonthreatening and convenient way for teachers to identify and analyze their question-phrasing behaviors and the cognitive levels of questions they use. The following steps are recommended for applying the ICI self-analysis approach:

1. Become familiar with question-phrasing techniques and four

cognitive levels of questions.

2. Teach an instructional episode or class using questioning behaviors with an audio or videotape being made.

3. Identify and analyze questioning behaviors by completing the analysis form (see Figure 1) and using the taped playback.

4. Repeat steps 2 and 3 if skills need further improvement.

A unique feature and advantage of the ICI approach as its two-dimensional analysis. The form includes two columns: "Occurrence," for recording the extent to which each component is evident, and "Effectiveness," for estimating the teacher's performance skill. These two kinds of data—descriptive and evaluative—contribute to a comprehensive analysis (68).

Another practical and beneficial method for teachers to gather information on their questioning behaviors is to have their students act as observers and data gatherers. As Hogg and Wilen suggest, students can be a practical and reliable source of feedback on teacher performance because they observe the teacher in action many hours each week (60). As observers, students provide a large sample, thereby reducing individual biases and increasing reliability. Systematic student observation of teachers is inexpensive, requires little time, and fits well into the classroom schedule. Secondary students can be easily trained to identify four cognitive levels of questions, perhaps using the Gallagher-Aschner approach, while intermediate students can become acquainted and practice with two levels such as convergent (closed) and divergent (open-ended) questions. A data gathering form incorporating space for students to record verbatim questions and to categorize them is quite simple to construct (60). Hunkins suggests several techniques to involve students in identifying and analyzing teacher questions (64).

CONCLUSION

Although there are conflicting findings and differing viewpoints in the research concerning the effective use of questions, most researchers, teachers, and educators would agree with DeGarmo's assertion that "to question well is to teach well" (32, p. 179). If teachers or students were polled to identify the factors they considered essential to good teaching, the common thread running through their responses would be the teacher's personal and intellectual relation to students through interaction. In a word, the common thread would be communication. Since communication is an essential of teaching, and questioning is an integral part of classroom verbal interaction, to a substantial degree teacher effectiveness is affected by questioning skill.

Figure 1
QUESTIONS AND QUESTIONING: ANALYSIS FORM*

Teacher _____ Class _____

Topic _____

ANALYSIS SCALES

Occurrence	Effectiveness
1. Not evident	1. Not effective
2. Slightly evident	2. Slightly effective
3. Moderately evident	3. Moderately effective
4. Quite evident	4. Quite effective
N Not Applicable	N Not applicable

PHRASING:	Extent	Appraisal
1. APPROPRIATE QUESTION LEVEL: Teacher used question at appropriate levels to achieve the objectives of the lesson.	____	____
2. ALLOWS THINKING TIME: Teacher paused sufficiently after asking higher-level questions in order to allow student thinking.	____	____
3. GROUP-INDIVIDUAL BALANCE: Teacher provided a balance between group-oriented and individual student questions.		
4. PARTICIPATION: Teacher encouraged participation by calling on volunteers and nonvolunteers.	____	____
5. FOLLOWUP QUESTIONS: Teacher followed up initial student responses with questions that encouraged students to complete, clarify, expand, or support.	____	____
6. APPROPRIATE VERBAL LEVEL: Teacher adjusted questions to the language and ability level of the students.	____	____

COGNITIVE LEVELS:	# Questions Asked	Est. % of Total
1. COGNITIVE-MEMORY: Narrow, closed questions that require students to recall or recognize information. Students recognized, recalled, defined, recounted, repeated, quoted, identified, or answered yes or no.	____	____
2. CONVERGENT: Narrow questions that require students to analyze and combine remembered information. Students translated, interpreted, related, explained, compared, contrasted, analyzed, associated, concluded, or summarized.	____	____
3. DIVERGENT: Broad, open-ended questions that require students to develop their own information or to view a topic from a new perspective. Students hypothesized, speculated, devised, inferred, predicted, implied, synthesized, or solved.	____	____
4. EVALUATIVE: Broad, open-ended questions that require students to judge, value, or choose with support from internal or external sources. Students opined, judged, rated per an explicit criterion, or made and defended a choice.	____	____

Total Number of Questions Asked ____

---

*Kindsvatter and Wilen (68, p. 313).

BIBLIOGRAPHY

1. Amidon, E. J., and Hunter, E. *Improving Teaching: Analyzing Verbal Interaction in the Classroom.* New York: Holt, Rinehart and Winston, 1966.
2. Anderson, H. H. "Domination and Social Integrative Behavior." In *Child Behavior and Development,* edited by R. G. Barker, J. S. Kounia, and H. F. Wright. New York: McGraw-Hill Book Co., 1943.
3. Arnold, D.S.; Atwood, R. K.; and Rogers, U. M. "An Investigation of the Relationships Among Question Level, Response Level, and Lapse Time." *School Science and Mathematics* 73 (October 1973): 591-94.
4. Ausubel, D. *The Psychology of Meaningful Verbal Learning.* New York: Grune and Stratton, 1963.
5. Barr, A. S. *Characteristic Differences in the Teaching Performance of Good and Poor Teachers of Social Studies.* Bloomington, Ill.: Public School Publishing Co., 1929.
6. Barth, J. L.; and Shermis, S. S. "A Study of Student Teachers' Effectiveness in Applying Inquiry Questioning Skills." *Journal of Social Studies Research* 4 (Summer 1980): 34-37.
7. Bellack, A. A., et al. *Language of the Classroom: Meanings Communicated in High School Teaching.* U.S. Office of Education, Department of Health, Education and Welfare, Cooperative Research Project No. 1497. New York: Teachers College Press, 1963.
8. Betts, G. H. *The Recitation.* Cambridge, Mass.: Houghton Mifflin Co., 1911.
9. Bloom, B. S., et al. *Taxonomy of Educational Objectives, Handbook I: Cognitive Domain.* New York: David McKay, 1956.
10. Blosser, P. E. "Review of Research: Teacher Questioning Behavior in Science Classrooms." Columbus, Ohio: ERIC Clearinghouse for Science, Mathematics and Environmental Education, December 1979. ED 184818.
11. Boocock, S., and Schild, E. O. *Simulation Games in Learning.* Beverly Hills, Calif.: Sage Publications, 1968.
12. Brophy, J. E., and Evertson, C. M. *Learning from Teaching.* Boston: Allyn and Bacon, 1976.
13. Bruner, J.; Goodnow, J. J.; and Austin, G. A. *A Study of Thinking.* New York: Science Editions, 1967.
14. Buggey, L. J. "A Study of the Relationship of Classroom Questions and Social Studies Achievement of Second Grade Children." Doctoral dissertation, University of Washington, 1971.
15. Burton, W. H. *The Nature and Direction of Learning.* New York: D. Appleton and Co., 1929.
16. Buttery, T. J., and Michalak, D. A. "Modifying Questioning Behavior via the Teaching Clinic Process." *Educational Research Quarterly* 3 (Summer 1978): 46-56.
17. Carin, A. A., and Sund, R. B. *Developing Questioning Techniques.* Columbus, Ohio: Charles E. Merrill Publishing Co., 1971.
18. Charters, W. W. *Methods of Teaching.* Chicago: Row, Peterson and Co., 1912.
19. Clegg, A. A., Jr. "Classroom Questions." In *The Encyclopedia of Education* (vol. 2), edited by Lee C. Deighton. New York: Macmillan, 1971.
20. _____; Farley, George T.; and Curran, Robert J. "Training Teachers to Analyze the Cognitive Level of Classroom Questioning." Research

Report No. 1, Applied Research Training Program, University of Massachusetts, 1967.

21. Colvin, S. S. "The Most Common Faults of Beginning High School Teachers." In *The Professional Preparation of High School Teachers*, Eighteenth Yearbook of the National Society for the Study of Education, edited by Guy M. Whipple and H. L. Miller. Bloomington, Ill.: Public School Publishing Co., 1919.

22. Corey, S. M. "Teachers Out-Talk the Pupils." *School Review* 48 (December 1940): 745-52.

23. _____, and Fahey, G. L. "Inferring Typed Pupil Mental Activity from Classroom Questions Asked." *Journal of Educational Psychology* 31 (February 1940): 94-102.

24. Cunningham, H. A. "Types of Thought Questions in General Science Textbooks and Laboratory Manuals." *General Science Quarterly* 9 (January 1925): 91-95.

25. Cunningham, R. T. "Developing Question-Asking Skills." In *Developing Teacher Competencies*, edited by J. Weigand. Englewood Cliffs, N.J.: Prentice-Hall, 1971.

26. _____. "A Descriptive Study Determining the Effects of a Method of Instruction Designed to Improve the Question Phrasing Practices of Prospective Elementary Teachers." Doctoral dissertation, Indiana University, 1968.

27. Curtis, F. D. "Types of Thought Questions in Textbooks of Science." *Science Education* 37 (September-October 1943): 60-69.

28. Crump, C. D. "Self-Instruction in the Art of Questioning in Intermediate-Grade Social Studies." Doctoral dissertation, Indiana University, 1969.

29. Davis, O. L. and Tinsley, D. C. "Cognitive Objectives Revealed by Classroom Questions Asked by Social Studies Student Teachers." *Peabody Journal of Education* 45 (1967): 21-26.

30. _____, and Hunkins, F. P. "Textbook Questions: What Thinking Processes Do They Foster?" *Peabody Journal of Education* 43 (March 1966); 285-92.

31. _____, et al. "Studying the Cognitive Emphasis of Teachers' Classroom Questions." *Educational Leadership* 26 (April 1969): 711.

32. DeGarmo, C. *Interest and Education.* New York: Macmillan, 1911.

33. Dewey, J. *How We Think.* Boston: D.C. Heath and Co., 1933.

34. Douce, H. L. "Raising the Cognitive Level of Teacher Questioning Behavior in Selected Schools." Doctoral dissertation, University of Washington, 1971.

35. Enokson, R. "A Simplified Teacher Question Classification Model." *Education* 94 (September/October 1933): 27-29.

36. Evenson, L. L. "Effects of High-Level Questions on Social Studies Achievement in Cooperative and Competitive Instructional Environments." Doctoral dissertation, Arizona State University, 1981.

37. Farley, G. T. and Clegg, A. A., Jr. "Increasing the Cognitive Level of Classroom Questions in Social Studies: An Application of Bloom's Taxonomy." Paper presented at American Educational Research Association Annual Meeting, Los Angeles, February 1969.

38. Fisher, F. L. "Influences of Reading and Discussion on the Attitudes of Fifth Graders Toward Indians." *Journal of Educational Research* 62 (November 1968): 130-34.

39. Fitch, J. G. *Lectures on Teaching.* New York: Macmillan, 1901.

40. Flanders, N. *Teacher Influence, Pupil Attitudes, and Achievement.*

U.S. Office of Education, Department of Health, Education and Welfare, Cooperative Research Project No. 397. Minneapolis: University of Minnesota, 1960.
41. Floyd, W. D. "An Analysis of the Oral Questioning Activity in Selected Colorado Primary Classrooms." Doctoral dissertation, Colorado State University, 1960.
42. Gall, M. D. "The Use of Questions in Teaching." *Review of Educational Research* 40 (1970): 707-21.
43. _____, et al. "Main Field Test Report: Minicourse 9—Thought Questions in the Intermediate Grades." Berkeley, Calif.: Far West Laboratory for Educational Research and Development, 1970.
44. _____, et al. *The Effects of Teacher Use of Questioning Techniques on Student Achievement and Attitudes.* San Francisco: Far West Laboratory for Educational Research and Development, 1975.
45. _____, et al. "Effects of Questioning Techniques and Recitation on Student Learning." *American Educational Research Journal* 15 (Spring 1978): 175-99.
46. _____, and Gillett, M. "The Discussion Method in Classroom Teaching." *Theory Into Practice* 19 (Spring 1980): 98-103.
47. Gallagher, J. J. *Productive Thinking of Gifted Children.* U.S. Office of Education, Department of Health, Education and Welfare, Cooperative Research Project No. 965. Urbana: University of Illinois, 1965.
48. _____, and Aschner, M. J. "A Preliminary Report on Analyses of Classroom Interaction." *Merrill-Palmer Quarterly* 9 (1963): 183-94.
49. Gambrell, L. B. "Think-time: Implications for Reading Instruction." *Reading Teacher* 34 (November 1980): 143-46.
50. Good, T. L., and Brophy, J. E. *Looking in Classrooms.* New York: Harper and Row, 1978.
51. Gordon, W. J. *Synectics.* New York: Harper and Row, 1961.
52. Green, J. "Editor's Note." *Clearing House* 40 (March 1966): 397.
53. Groisser, P. *How to Use the Fine Art of Questioning.* Englewood Cliffs, N.J.: Prentice-Hall, 1964.
54. Guilford, J. P. "The Structure of Intellect." *Psychological Bulletin* 53 (July 1956): 267-93.
55. Guszak, F. J. "Teacher Questioning and Reading." *Reading Teacher* 21 (December 1967): 227-34.
56. Hamilton, S. *Recitation.* Philadelphia: J. P. Lippincott Co., 1906.
57. Hargie, O. D. "The Importance of Teacher Questions in the Classroom." *Educational Research* 20 (February 1978): 99-102.
58. Hassler, D. M. K. "A Study to Investigate the Effects of Wait-Time and Questioning Strategies in the Oral Language Behaviors of Teachers and Students During Children's Literature Discussions in Language Arts." Doctoral dissertation, Pennsylvania State University, 1980.
59. Hoetker, W. J., and Ahlbrand, W. P. "The Persistence of the Recitation." *American Educational Research Journal* 6 (March 1969): 145-67.
60. Hogg, J., and Wilen, W. "Evaluating Teachers' Questions: A New Dimension in Students' Assessment of Instruction." *Phi Delta Kappan* 58 (November 1976): 281-82.
61. Houston, V. M. "Improving the Quality of Classroom Questions and Questioning." *Educational Administration and Supervision* 24 (January 1938): 17-28.
62. Hudgins, B. B., and Ahlbrand, W. P., Jr. *A Study of Classroom Interaction and Thinking.* St. Louis: Central Midwestern Regional

Educational Laboratory, 1967.
63. Hunkins, F. P. "The Influence of Analysis and Evaluation Questions on Various Levels of Achievement." *Journal of Experimental Education* 38 (Winter 1969): 45-58.
64. _____. *Involving Students in Questioning.* Boston: Allyn and Bacon, 1976.
65. _____. *Questioning Strategies and Techniques.* Boston: Allyn and Bacon, 1972.
66. Hyman, R. T. *Strategic Questioning.* Englewood Cliffs, N.J.: Prentice-Hall, 1979.
67. _____. *Ways of Teaching.* Philadelphia: J. B. Lippincott Co., 1974.
68. Kindsvatter, R., and Wilen, W. "Improving Classroom Instruction: A Self- and Shared-Analysis Approach." In *Teaching in Higher Education: Readings for Faculty,* edited by S. C. Scholl and S. C. Inglis. Columbus, Ohio: Ohio Board of Regents, 1977.
69. Kleinman, G. "Teachers' Questions and Student Understanding of Science." *Journal of Research in Science Teaching* 3 (December 1965): 307-17.
70. Kniep, W. M., and Grossman, G. "Effects of High-Level Questions in Competitive and Cooperative Environments on the Achievement of Selective Social Studies Concepts." *Journal of Educational Research* 73 (November/December 1979): 82-85.
71. Konya, B. A. "The Effects of Higher- and Lower-Order Teacher Questions on the Frequency and Types of Student Verbalizations." Doctoral dissertation, University of Tennessee, 1972.
72. Ladas, H., and Osti, L. "Asking Questions: A Strategy for Teachers." *High School Journal* 56 (January 1973): 174-80.
73. Ladd, G. T. "Determining the Level of Inquiry in Teachers' Questions." Doctoral dissertation, Indiana University, 1969.
74. Land, M. L. "Teacher Clarity and Cognitive Level of Questions: Effects on Learning." *Journal of Experimental Education* 49 (Fall 1980): 48-51.
75. Levin, T., with Lang, R. *Effective Instruction.* Washington, D.C.: ASCD, 1981.
76. Malvern, K. T. "The Effect of High Cognitive Questioning Techniques on Student Achievement after Teaching Retraining in Questioning Strategies." Doctoral dissertation, Rutgers University, 1980.
77. McNamara, D. R. "Teaching Skill: The Question of Questioning." *Educational Research* 23 (February 1981): 104-9.
78. Medley, D. M. "The Effectiveness of Teachers." In *Research on Teaching: Concepts, Findings, and Implications,* edited by P. L. Peterson and H. L. Walberg. Berkeley: McCutchan, 1979.
79. Mills, S. R., et al. "Correspondence Between Teacher Questions and Student Answers in Classroom Discourse." *Journal of Experimental Education* 48 (Spring 1980): 194-204.
80. Morrison, T. "Methods of Instruction." *Barnard's American Journal of Education* 9 (September 1860): 294-320.
81. Moyer, J. R. "An Exploratory Study of Questioning in the Instructional Processes of Selected Elementary Schools." Doctoral dissertation, Columbia University, 1965.
82. Oliver, D., and Shaver, J. P. *Teaching Public Issues in the High School.* Boston: Houghton Mifflin Co., 1966.
83. Pagliaro, M. M. "The Effect of Cooperating Teacher Questioning Behaviors on Facilitating the Questioning Behaviors of Student Teachers." Doctoral dissertation, Fordham University, 1978.

84. Pate, R. T., and Bremer, N. H. "Guiding Learning Through Skillful Questioning." *Elementary School Journal* 67 (1967): 417-22.

85. Pfeiffer, I., and Davis, O. L., Jr. "Teacher-Made Examinations: What Kinds of Thinking Do They Demand?" *NASSP Bulletin* 49 (September 1965): 1-10.

86. Psencik, L. F. "Some Relationships Between Attitude, Verbal Behavior, and Cognitive Level of Classroom Questions of Secondary American History." Doctoral dissertation, Texas A & M University, 1971.

87. Riegle, R. P. "The Logic of Classroom Questions." Doctoral dissertation, Ohio State University, 1974.

88. Rogers, C. *Client-Centered Therapy*. Boston: Houghton Mifflin Co., 1971.

89. Rosenshine, B. *Teaching Behaviors and Student Achievement*. London: National Foundation for Educational Research in England and Wales, 1971.

90. _____. "Classroom Instruction." In *The Psychology of Teaching Methods*, edited by W. L. Gage. Chicago: University of Chicago Press, 1976.

91. _____. "Content, Time, and Direct Instruction." In *Research on Teaching: Concepts, Findings, and Implications*, edited by P. L. Peterson and H. L. Walberg. Berkeley: McCutchan, 1979.

92. Ross, Rev. W. "Methods of Instruction." Barnard's *American Journal of Education* 9 (September 1860): 367-79.

93. Rothkopf, E. Z. "Variable Adjunct Question Schedules, Interpersonal Interaction, and Incidental Learning from Written Material." *Journal of Educational Psychology* 63 (April 1972): 87-92.

94. Rowe, M. B. "Wait-Time and Reward as Instructional Variables, Their Influence on Language, Logic, and Fate Control: Part One— Wait Time." *Journal of Research on Science Teaching* 11 (1974): 81-94.

95. Sadker, M., and Sadker, D. "Questioning Skills." In *Classroom Teaching Skills: A Handbook*, edited by James M. Cooper. Lexington, Mass.: D. C. Heath and Co., 1977.

96. Sanders, N. M. *Classroom Questions: What Kinds?* New York: Harper and Row, 1966.

97. Savage, T. V. "A Study of the Relationship of Classroom Questions and Social Studies Achievement of Fifth-Grade Children." Doctoral dissertation, University of Washington, 1972.

98. Shaftel, F., and Shaftel, G. *Role Playing for Social Values: Decision Making in the Social Studies*. Englewood Cliffs, N.J.: Prentice-Hall, 1967.

99. Simon A., and Boyer, E. G., eds. *Mirrors for Behavior III: An Anthology of Observation Instruments*. Philadelphia: Research for Better Schools, 1974.

100. Smith, B. O., and Meuz, M. *A Study of the Logic of Teaching*. Urbana: Bureau of Educational Research, University of Illinois, 1962.

101. _____. "Conceptual Frameworks for Analysis of Classroom Social Interaction: Comments on Four Papers." *Journal of Experimental Education* 30 (June 1962): 325-26.

102. Soar, R. S. *Follow Through Classroom Process Measurement and Pupil Growth (1970-71): Final Report*. Gainesville: College of Education, University of Florida, 1973.

103. Stallings, J., and Kaskowitz, D. *Follow-Through Classroom Observation Evaluation*. Menlo Park, Calif.: Stanford Research Institute, 1974.

104. Stevens, R. *The Question as a Means of Efficiency in Instruction: A Critical Study of Classroom Practice*. New York: Teachers College, Columbia University, 1912.

105. Suchman, J. R. *The Elementary School Training Program in Scientific Inquiry*. Report to the U.S. Office of Education, Project Title VII, Project 216. Urbana: University of Illinois, 1962.

106. Taba, H.; Levine, S.; and Elzey, F. F. *Thinking in Elementary School Children*. U.S. Office of Education, Department of Health, Education and Welfare, Cooperative Research Project No. 1574. San Francisco: San Francisco State College, 1964.

107. Tinsley, D. C., and Davis, O. L., Jr. "Questions Used by Secondary Student Teachers to Guide Discussion and Testing in Social Studies: A Study in Planning." *Journal of Teacher Education* 22 (Spring 1971): 59-65.

108. Weil, M., and Joyce, B. *Information Processing Models of Teaching*. Englewood Cliffs, N.J.: Prentice-Hall, 1978.

109. _____, and _____. *Social Models of Teaching*. Englewood Cliffs, N.J.: Prentice-Hall, 1978.

110. _____; _____; and Kluwin, B. *Personal Models of Teaching*. Englewood Cliffs, N.J.: Prentice-Hall, 1978.

111. Welch, H. E. "The Effects of a Self-Instructional Learning Program on the Oral Questioning Behavior of Social Studies Student Teachers." Doctoral dissertation, East Texas State University, 1976.

112. Wilen, W. "The Preferences of American History Students for the Cognitive Levels of Teachers' Verbal Questioning Behavior and the Relationship of Preferences to Achievement." Doctoral dissertation, Pennsylvania State University, 1973.

113. _____; Dietrich, R.; and Owen, D. "A Study: Guidelines for Improving Questioning Techniques." *OCSS Review* 13 (Spring 1977): 16-22.

114. _____, and Searles, J. E. "Teachers' Questioning Behavior: Students' Preferences and the Relationship of Preferences to Achievement." *Education* 98 (Winter 1977): 237-45.

115. Wilson, M. M. "Processing Strategies of Average and Below Average Readers Answering Factual and Inferential Questions on Three Equivalent Passages." *Journal of Reading Behavior* 11 (Fall 1979): 234-45.

116. Winne, P. H., and Marx, R. W. "Perceptual Problem Solving." In *Research on Teaching: Concepts, Findings, and Implications*, edited by P. L. Peterson and H. L. Walberg. Berkeley: McCutchan, 1979.

117. _____. "Experiments Relating Teachers' Use of Higher Cognitive Questions to Student Achievement." *Review of Educational Research* 49 (Winter 1979): 13-50.

118. Withall, J. "The Development of a Technique for the Measurement of Social-Emotional Climate in Classrooms." *Journal of Experimental Education* 17 (March 1949): 347-61.

119. Wright, C. J:. and Nuthall, G. "Relationships Between Teacher Behaviors and Pupil Achievement in Three Elementary Science Lessons." *American Educational Research Journal* 7 (1970): 477-93.

120. Wright, L. M. P. "The Effect of Microteaching Utilizing Feedback and Models on the Development of Questioning Skills." Doctoral dissertation, University of Maryland, 1979.

121. Zoch, F. R. "The Effects of an Individualized In-service Program on Teacher Questioning and Student Verbal Participation." Doctoral dissertation, University of Houston, 1970.